Patch Goes Home

This is a story about a cat called Patch.
He was a nice black cat with white paws and a white
patch on his chest. He lived with a family called Smith.
Mr and Mrs Smith had two children. They were called
Margaret and Jack and they were very fond of the cat.
They called him Patch because of the white patch on
his chest.

One day Margaret and Jack were sitting on the steps
of their house. They were watching the cat washing his
face.

"Patch is clever," Jack said. "He can wash his own
face."

The cat washed round behind his ears, licking his paw to make it wet.

"He washes behind his ears too," said Margaret. "You don't do that. The cat is cleverer than you."

"He isn't," said Jack, and he tried to pull Margaret's hair. Then Mrs Smith came out to see what they were doing. Jack told her what Margaret said, and Mrs Smith replied:

"I think you really can wash behind your ears! You just forget sometimes. But a cat can do a lot of things you can't do. He can jump very high, and he can see in the dark."

"He can catch mice too," said Jack.

Just then Mr Smith came home from work and the children ran to meet him.

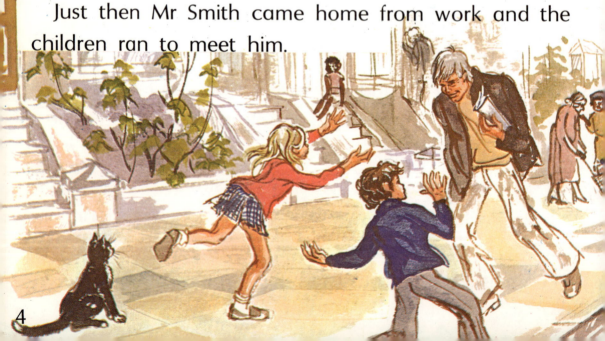

4

When they were all back in the house Mr Smith told them he had got a new job.

"It's in a new factory in Newtown," he said. "It's a long way from here so we'll have to find a new house."

Mr and Mrs Smith went to look at lots of new houses till they found one that they liked. It had plenty of room for everyone. Mr Smith said it was near his new job. Mrs Smith liked the kitchen. Margaret liked the bathroom and Jack liked the little garden.

Mr Smith said they would take the house. Patch sat on a chair and purred, so they all said: "I wonder if Patch will like the house too?"

One Saturday morning the removal men came with a big van and put all the furniture in it. They took the chairs and tables and the beds, and the television and the toys. They took Patch's bed too.

When the house was empty Mrs Smith swept the floor and put all the rubbish in the bin.

Patch went round the empty house, looking very puzzled. He didn't like it at all. Then Mr Smith put him in a basket with a lid, and they all went away to the new house in a taxi. Patch couldn't see where they were going and he mewed all the time.

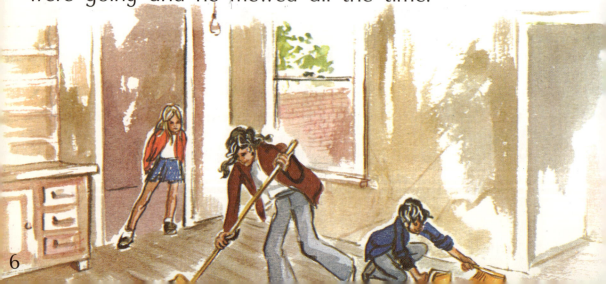

When they came to the new house they helped the removal men to put everything in the right place.

They let Patch out of his basket. He went round the house, sniffing at everything. Then he went out into the garden.

Margaret and Jack went to play in the garden too. Soon Mrs Smith called:

"Come and get something to eat before you go to bed." They were just running in when Jack said: "Where's the cat?"

They stopped and called "Patch, Patch! Come on puss! Come on puss!" But the cat never came.

They looked all over the garden and all over the house, but they couldn't find the cat. They looked under the beds and on all the chairs and under the television, but they couldn't find the cat anywhere.

The children were very worried.

"Maybe he'll come back later," said Mrs Smith. "Now you go to bed and don't worry." Margaret and Jack went to bed but they lay for a long time wondering where Patch was.

Then Jack had a brainwave. "I think Patch has gone back to our old house," he said.

Margaret told him not to be silly. She said Patch did not know where the old house was.

Then they fell asleep because they were very tired.

Next morning Jack told his mummy and daddy about his brainwave. Mr Smith said:

"What a good idea! You and I will get the bus and go back to the old house, just to see."

So Jack and his daddy took the basket with the lid and they went back to their old house. When they got there they went up the stairs, and what do you think they saw?

They saw the cat sitting outside the door of their old house. He was mewing very sadly, but when he saw Jack he stood up and started to purr.
Jack picked him up and stroked his fur and said:

"Silly old puss. We've got a new house now and we don't live in this house any more."

They put Patch in the basket and went home in the bus.

When they got home Mrs Smith and Margaret were very happy to see the cat again.

Mrs Smith said:

"We must put butter on his paws, and then he will always come back to this house."

Mr Smith said:

"It was very clever of Jack to know where to look for Patch."

But Margaret said:

"It was very clever of Patch to find his way back to our old house. I wonder how he did it? He couldn't see out of the basket when we went in the taxi."

They all looked at Patch, and Patch just sat on Margaret's knee and purred and purred.

On The Moon

The moon is very far away. A space-ship takes about five days to get there.

It is very quiet on the moon.

The ground is covered with grey dust and big stones.

There is no air on the moon and there is no water.

So there are no trees, and no flowers, and no animals.

Nothing lives on the moon.

When men go to the moon
they have to wear space-suits. They have
to take water and oxygen with them.
They have to take food to eat too, because
there is nothing to eat on the moon.

When a man is on the moon he can jump
quite high. But he soon gets tired because
his space-suit is very heavy.

The first man who landed on the moon was
Neil Armstrong. Here is a picture of Neil
Armstrong on the moon in his space-suit.
You can see the space-ship behind him.

Would you like to go to the moon some day?

A Sensible Girl

It was Saturday morning and Jill was thinking about what she was going to do. First she was going to go to the shops with her mummy and little Sandra and the baby. Then she was going to play with her friend Penny. In the afternoon Daddy was going to take them all to the zoo. It was going to be a lovely day.

Jill sat on the step of her house and thought about the zoo. She liked the zoo very much. She liked the monkeys and the penguins and the polar bears and the sea lions. She liked the lions and tigers too, but she was glad that they were in behind big iron bars.

The last time she was at the zoo she had a ride on the elephant. She remembered how funny it felt being so high up. She remembered how the elephant waved his trunk about.

She was still thinking about the elephant when she heard a noise inside the house. She heard Sandra crying and her mummy calling. She ran in to see what had happened.

Sandra was lying on the floor. Jill saw a chair and a broken bottle of lemonade beside her. Sandra was crying and her face was very white. One of her legs looked funny and her hand had a cut in it. Mummy was kneeling beside her and looking very worried.

"Sandra has hurt her leg," Mummy said. "I'll have to take her to hospital."

Jill sat down on the floor beside Sandra. Mummy went and telephoned for an ambulance. Then Jill said:

"What about me and baby? Can we come too?"

Her mummy said nothing for a minute. Then she said:

"I don't think there is time to get baby ready. Could you be a clever girl and look after him until I come back? I'll tell Mrs Wilson next door and she will come in beside you."

Jill felt a little bit frightened. She had never been in the house without her mummy or her daddy. But she said "All right" because she was the biggest girl in the family. Jill's mummy went and rang Mrs Wilson's bell. Mrs Wilson came to the door.

"Mrs Wilson," Jill's mummy said, "can you come in and look after Jill and the baby? Sandra has hurt her leg and I'll have to take her to hospital."

"Yes, of course," said Mrs Wilson. "Just wait a minute till I switch off the kettle."

Then the bell rang in Jill's house. It was the ambulance men for Sandra. They brought in a stretcher and they put a nice red blanket round Sandra and put her on the stretcher. Mummy said:

"We won't be long. Take care of baby. Mrs Wilson is just coming in," and she went away with the ambulance men. Mrs Wilson came in and went into the kitchen.

Baby had just had a bath. He was lying on the rug,
kicking his legs. Jill thought:

"I must get something warm for him," so she went
and got some clothes for him. He was quite good
and let her dress him.

Then she saw all the broken glass on the floor.
She lifted baby up and put him in his play-pen.
She gave him a rattle and some little boxes to play
with.

Mrs Wilson came in from the kitchen. She said Jill was very clever to dress baby and put him in his play-pen.

"If he crawled over the floor he would cut himself on the glass," said Jill.

"Let's clean up all the broken glass,"said Mrs Wilson. So Jill got a broom and they swept up all the glass and then they cleaned up the lemonade with a cloth.

"I must go back to the kitchen now,"said Mrs Wilson. "I've got to get your dinner ready. "Can you stay with baby by yourself?"

Jill said she would stay with him. Mrs Wilson went to peel the potatoes and Jill played with the baby.

Jill wondered how Sandra was getting on.
She went to the window to see if her mummy was
coming back. She had been away for a long time.
Jill gave the baby a biscuit and she had one herself.
She looked at her comic.

Mrs Wilson came back into the room.

"Are you all right?" she asked. Jill said:

"Yes, but I wonder when Mummy is coming back?"
Mrs Wilson said she wouldn't be long.

Then the telephone rang. Jill wondered who it was.
Mrs Wilson lifted the phone and said "Hullo?" Then
she handed it to Jill. Jill heard a voice saying, "Hullo,
Jill. Are you all right?"

It was Jill's mummy and she was telephoning from
the hospital. She said Sandra had to have an
X-ray and the doctor was going to put her leg
in plaster.

"Is baby all right?" mummy asked, and Jill said he
was quite happy. Mummy said she would soon be
home, and Jill said "Cheerio" and put down the phone.

But just then baby started to cry. He cried and
cried. He wouldn't play with his toys. Jill tried to
make him laugh but he just went on crying.
Mrs Wilson came and lifted him up but he wouldn't
stop. Jill didn't know what to do. She wished her
mummy would come.

Then she heard someone at the door. It was her
mummy and the ambulance man with Sandra.
He put Sandra down on the couch. One of her legs
was in plaster.

When baby saw his mummy he stopped crying
at once. Jill ran to her and said:

"Oh, mummy, I'm so glad you're back."

Mummy said:

"So am I, and I think you are a very clever girl.
You were mummy for a whole hour."

When her daddy came home for his dinner he
was very surprised to see Sandra with her leg in
plaster. Jill told him about the accident and how
she had to stay with baby and Mrs Wilson.

Her mummy said:

"Sandra was brave in the hospital, but Jill was very brave too. She looked after baby till I came back."

Jill's daddy lifted her up.

"What a sensible little girl we've got," he said. "Sandra and mummy have to stay at home, but I think you and I will go to the zoo this afternoon. Would you like that?"

Jill said: "Oh yes!"

All at once it was a lovely day after all.

Something to Make
CHOCOLATE CRISPIES

It is very easy to make Chocolate Crispies.
You will need these things:
One 2-ounce bar of plain chocolate
One teacup of corn flakes
Half a teacup of raisins

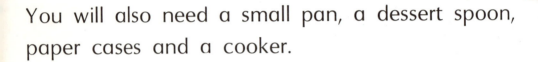

You will also need a small pan, a dessert spoon,
paper cases and a cooker.

What to do:

Break up the chocolate into little bits.
Put them in the pan and heat them until the chocolate
is melted. Do not let the chocolate get too hot.
Stir in the corn flakes and raisins.
Put a spoonful of the mixture into each paper case.
Leave them to cool.

Chocolate is made from a plant that grows in Africa.

Corn Flakes are made from a plant that grows
in America.

Raisins come from Australia.

So the things in your chocolate crispies come from
all round the world.

Big ships bring them to our country.

Jack and the Beanstalk

Once upon a time a poor woman lived in a little house with her son Jack. The woman had one cow and she kept the cow in the field beside her house.

One day Jack's mother said to him:

"Jack, I've got no money left. I can't buy any more food for us to eat. You must take our cow to the market and sell her."

Jack was very sad but he did what he was told. He put a rope round the cow's neck and he went away to the market in the town. His mother waited all day for him to come back.

At last she saw him coming along the road. She ran to meet him and called out.

"Did you get a lot of money for the cow?"

Jack pulled a little bag out of his pocket and gave
it to his mother. She opened it and looked inside.
It was not full of money.
It was full of beans.
"Where is the money?" his mother asked.
"I haven't got any money," said Jack.
"A man gave me the beans for the cow and he said
they were magic beans."
Jack's mother was very angry.
"You are a silly boy," she said.
"Now we have no cow and no money. You must go
to bed without any supper." She took the bag of beans
and she threw them on to the ground. Jack went to bed.
He was very tired and he fell asleep at once.

The next morning Jack's mother got up and went to look out of the window. She got a very big surprise. She couldn't see out of the window, because something was growing in front of it. She ran to the door to see what it was.

A big green plant was growing out of the ground. It was growing just where the beans had fallen. It was a great big beanstalk.

Jack's mother called to him:

"Jack, come and see this. Come and see this." Jack jumped out of bed and came running to the door.

The beanstalk was the biggest one he had ever seen. He looked up. He couldn't see the top of it. The beanstalk went up and up into the air.

He said to his mother:

"I'm going to climb up to see what is at the top."

So he went and put on his clothes and had his breakfast, and then he began to climb. He climbed up and up till he got to the top of the beanstalk.

He was very surprised at what he saw. He found some fields and a road. The road went up a hill, and at the end of the road there was a big castle. Jack went along the road and he met an old man.

"Who lives in that castle?" Jack asked.

"It is a giant," the old man said. "Don't go near, for if he finds you near the castle he will kill you."

"I'm not afraid of a giant," said Jack, and he walked on.

He did not meet anyone else until he was nearly at the door of the castle. Then the door opened and a woman came out. When she saw Jack she looked very frightened and called to him:

"What are you doing here? What do you want?"

"I'm Jack," said Jack. "I've come up the beanstalk and I'm looking for something to take back to my mother."

"Run away at once," the woman said. "My husband is a giant and if he finds you he will kill you."

Just then Jack heard someone singing in a very loud voice:

"Fee fi fo fum,
I smell an Englishman."

"That's my husband," the woman said. "Come in quickly and I'll hide you." So she pulled Jack into the kitchen of the castle and hid him in a big oven.

When the giant came in she brought his dinner. After he had eaten it all up, he shouted:

"Bring me my bag of gold." So his wife brought a big bag and put it down on the table in front of him. The

giant was just going to open the bag when the woman let all the dishes fall. Crash!

The giant got up to see what the noise was. Jack jumped out of the oven, grabbed the bag and ran out of the castle door as fast as he could.

He ran down the road and past the fields, till he came to the top of the beanstalk. He slid quickly down to the bottom and ran into the house.

"See what I've got, mother," he called, and he emptied out all the gold money on the table.

His mother was so surprised she couldn't say anything. She put the money back in the bag and hid it away.

Jack and his mother had plenty of money to buy good food now. They got another cow and they were very happy. Then one day they spent the last gold penny.

34

"I must go up the beanstalk again," Jack said, and he climbed up once more. He walked along the road and up to the castle, and he met the giant's wife.

"Go away," she said. "The giant is coming for his dinner and he will kill you because you stole his gold."

Then Jack heard the giant singing again:

"Fee fi fo fum,

I smell an Englishman."

"Quick! Come in and I'll hide you," the woman said, and she pulled Jack into the kitchen and hid him in a great big pot. She put the lid on but she left a little space and Jack saw the giant coming in.

The giant got his dinner and then he shouted:

"Bring me my goose that lays golden eggs." His wife brought in a big grey goose and put it on the table.

"Lay a golden egg for me," said the giant, and the goose laid a beautiful golden egg.

Just then the giant's wife called:

"Help me! My pan of fat is on fire!" The giant went to help his wife and Jack jumped out of the pot, grabbed the goose and ran out of the door. But the goose was frightened and made a loud noise and the giant heard her. He came after Jack, waving a big club.

Jack raced back to the top of the beanstalk. He slid quickly down, grabbed his big axe and chopped the beanstalk right through. Down fell the beanstalk and down fell the giant. CRASH! Then everything was very quiet. The giant was dead.

Jack took the goose to his mother and they made a little house for her. Every day she laid a beautiful golden egg and Jack and his mother became rich and lived happily ever after.

How to grow Grass

It is very easy to grow grass in school.

You will need:
One egg box
One small packet of grass seed
Some soil
Some water and a little watering-can.

What to do:
Put some of the soil in the egg box.
Spread the soil out flat, then scatter some
grass seed over it.
Cover the seed with some more soil, then sprinkle
water over the soil until it is damp.
Do not make it too wet.

Put the box on a window-sill. Keep the soil damp.
Soon you will see the grass growing up through
the soil.

Pull out one of the blades of grass.
What colour is the part that was above the soil?
What colour is the part that was below the soil?

A Recipe for
Coconut Ice

4 ounces icing sugar   1 egg white
4 ounces coconut   a little red colouring

What to do:

1. Put the icing sugar in a bowl.
2. Make it smooth with a wooden spoon.
3. Add the coconut and mix it with the sugar.
4. Put the egg-white in a cup and beat it with a fork.
5. Add the egg-white to the sugar and coconut and mix it well. It will be very stiff, so take plenty of time.

6. Put half of the mixture on the table and roll it into a square.

7. Add 4 drops of red colouring to the rest of the mixture and mix well. The mixture will be pink.

8. Roll out the pink mixture.

9. Put the pink bit on top of the white bit and press them together.

10. Leave it to get hard.

11. Cut it into small squares.

12. Eat it.

 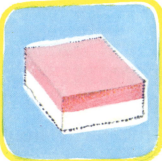

Coconut is made from the inside of a big nut.

The coconuts grow on a tree called a palm.

They grow in hot countries far away.

Here is a coconut palm.

The Wind

I am the wind.
I am very strong.
I blow over the sky
I make the big black clouds go by.

I am the wind.
I blow over the grass
and the flowers bend low when I pass.

I am the wind.
I blow over the sea.
I make big waves
and the waves run away from me.

I am very strong,
I am the wind.

New Words

The next story is about South America.
It has some new words in it.

The story is about **twins**. Twins are two children
who were born at the same time and have the same
mother. Sometimes they look very like each other.
You can see the twins on page 45.

The story tells you about a **canyon**. You can see
a canyon on page 52. It is deep and has steep sides.
There is a river at the bottom.

The story tells you that the twins were called
Carlo and **Pedro**. Can you say their names?

The story tells you that Pedro was wearing a **cloak**.
A cloak is like a long coat, but it does not have
any sleeves. You can see Pedro wearing his cloak
on page 50.

The story tells you about **stepping-stones**.
Stepping-stones are stones in a river. You can
step on them to cross the water without getting wet.
You can see stepping-stones in the picture on page 51.

The story tells you about **mountains**.
A mountain is a very high hill. Sometimes mountains
have snow on top of them. You can see mountains
with snow on them in the picture on page 43.

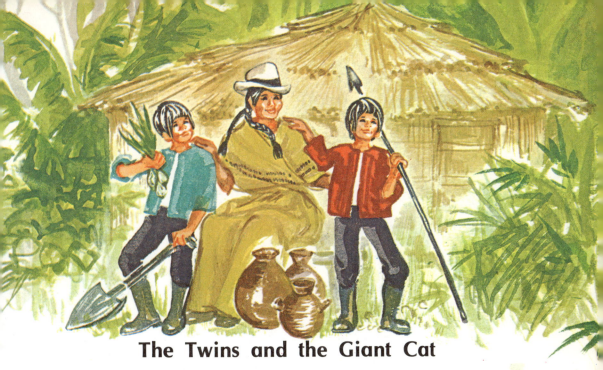

The Twins and the Giant Cat
A Tale from South America

A long, long time ago a woman lived beside a canyon in the mountains. She lived in a little house with her two sons who were twins. They looked very like each other.

They were the same size.

They had the same hair.

They had the same eyes.

Their voices were the same.

One of the boys was called Carlo and the other was called Pedro. Carlo always wore red clothes and Pedro always wore blue ones, so that people could tell one twin from the other.

Carlo was a hunter and went out every day to the forest. Pedro liked working with trees and plants. He grew corn and he chopped wood for his mother's fire in winter.

One day Carlo came home from the forest and found his mother and Pedro with the door locked. He knocked on the door and called:

"It is Carlo. Let me in." Then Pedro came and let him in.

"What is wrong?" Carlo asked. "Why do you have the door locked?"

Pedro said:

"Today when I was chopping wood I suddenly heard a terrible noise – like a cat, but much louder. I ran to the house, went inside and locked the door. I looked out

through the little window and I saw a great big cat. It was a giant cat. The giant cat said he had come to be king of the forest. He said we must all do what he told us, or else he would eat us up. Then he went away."

Their mother said:

"Oh, what shall we do? It will be terrible to have a big cat for our king."

Carlo said:

"Mother, go to bed and rest. Pedro and I will sit and talk by the fire."

So Carlo and Pedro sat by the fire and talked for a long time.

In the morning they said:

"Mother, we are going to show the giant cat that he is not the king of the forest. You must help us. If he comes back, do not tell him that you have two sons. Tell him you have only one."

So that day Carlo went out as usual with his bow and arrow, but he did not go far away. Pedro stayed inside the hut. Soon the giant cat came crashing through the trees, spitting and howling. Carlo heard him and he ran into the house and locked the door just in time.

"Mi-aa-ow," the giant cat called. "I am the king of the forest."

Then the boy's mother said:

"Oh, big cat, do not be cruel to me. I am a poor woman with only one son."

"Mi-aa-ow," said the giant cat again. "I want to see your son. Is he at home?"

"Yes," Carlo said, and he opened the door a little, so that the cat could see him. "I am a hunter," Carlo said, "and I want to see how fast you can run. If you can run faster than me, you can be our king."

"Of course I can run faster than you," said the giant cat.

"Then let us have a race," said Carlo. "Tomorrow morning, come to the edge of the canyon. I shall be there to meet you and we shall see who is the fastest runner."

"Mi-aa-ow," said the giant cat. "I'll be there. But I'll beat you," and he ran off into the forest.

Then their mother said:

"You cannot run faster than the big cat." But Carlo said:

"Mother, don't be afraid. Pedro and I have a good plan."

Then he said to Pedro:

"Pedro, you must go at once to the other side of the canyon. It is a long way so you must start now. Take a big knife and some food. Put on some of my clothes so that you look just like me. Put on this red cloak to hide your jacket. You can sleep in the cloak at night."

Pedro did all the things that Carlo told him, and he set off. He came to the side of the canyon and he climbed down. He looked around for the giant cat but it was not there.

Pedro found some stepping-stones over the river and he had a rest and something to eat. Then he climbed up the other side. When he reached the top it was getting dark, so he wrapped himself in his cloak and went to sleep under a tree.

The next morning he awoke early and had some breakfast. Then he went and stood on the edge of the canyon just as Carlo had told him.

Carlo was already standing on the other side, waiting for the cat to come.

Soon the giant cat came out of the forest. He was spitting and howling.

"Mi-aa-ow," he said. "Where shall we run our race?"

"I shall race you to the other side of the canyon," Carlo said.

"That's easy," the giant cat said, and he went off, scrambling down over the stones. Carlo started to run the race, and then came back and sat down.

After about five minutes the giant cat reached the other side. He was huffing and puffing. And there was Pedro! The cat was so surprised he couldn't say anything. He thought it was Carlo, because he didn't know there were two boys.

"Hullo," Pedro said. "You took a long time."

"I can go much faster than that," said the giant cat. "BACK AGAIN!" he shouted, and he set off, making a lot of dust. He scrambled down to the river, swam across, and scrambled up the other side. "I've beaten you this time!" he called.

But there was Carlo waiting for him.

"Is that the best you can do?" said Carlo.

"NO!" said the giant cat, "BACK AGAIN!" And off he went again, at a great speed, kicking up a lot of stones. He reached the other side in only two minutes. And there was Pedro!

The giant cat thought it was Carlo again. He felt very
tired and his fur was covered with mud.

"How can you go so fast?" he said to Pedro.

"Oh," said Pedro, "I had plenty of time."

"BACK AGAIN!" shouted the cat. He went off so fast
that it was like the wind blowing. He went as fast as he
could. But when he climbed up over the edge of the
canyon, there was Carlo.

The giant cat lay down. Carlo came and said to him: "You are not the king of the forest. I am faster and stronger than you. You must do what I tell you. You must go away into the mountains and stay there for ever."

So the giant cat went away into the mountains. He never came back to frighten the people in the forest, and the woman lived happily with her two clever sons.

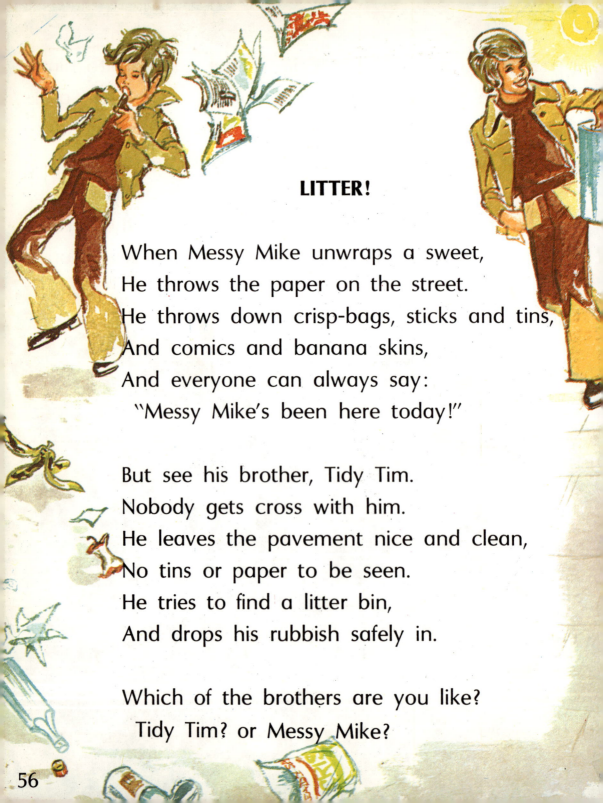

LITTER!

When Messy Mike unwraps a sweet,
He throws the paper on the street.
He throws down crisp-bags, sticks and tins,
And comics and banana skins,
And everyone can always say:
  "Messy Mike's been here today!"

But see his brother, Tidy Tim.
Nobody gets cross with him.
He leaves the pavement nice and clean,
No tins or paper to be seen.
He tries to find a litter bin,
And drops his rubbish safely in.

Which of the brothers are you like?
  Tidy Tim? or Messy Mike?